D1713611

All That Remains

Brian Fanelli

ISBN 978-1-936373-46-8
Published in the United States by Unbound Content, LLC,
Englewood, NJ.
Cover art: In the Crypt © 2013 Jeffrey Smyers
Author photo: © 2013 Susan Jaffer
The poems in this collection are all original and previously
unpublished with the exception of those listed in the credits
page at the end of the volume.

All That Remains
First edition 2013

For my father

Table of Contents

Dive

I stood behind Melissa Maroon,
stared at her budding curves,
bright pink bathing suit,
sun-kissed legs that climbed
step by step to the top of the dive.
She smiled at her giggling girlfriends,
pinched her nose, made little splash,
surfaced with a wink that made me blush.

When my turn came, my teeth chattered,
my weak heart sunk.
Melissa shouted, *Go, Bri, Go!*
How did she know my name?

My dive had to be just right,
a perfect splash, high fives from the guys.
Then maybe she'd see beyond
my chicken arms, chicken legs,
zits dotting my nose,
bony hips barely holding up my bathing suit.

I clenched my fists, closed my eyes,
bounced once, jumped off.
Water stung my belly, burned my eyes.
I pushed my body out of the pool,
collapsed next to Melissa's giggling girlfriends.
She glared at them, walked over to me, and said,
That was the best belly flop I've ever seen!

I gave my towel back to her,
strutted to the ladder for another chance.
I forgot about my bony hips,
bony arms, bony legs.
This time I performed a dive perfect enough
to earn a peck on the cheek from the girl,
a high five from all the guys.

The Quiet Fan

Cobain howled through my speakers,
his voice raw enough to rattle walls.
I tried to mimic the music on my own
baby blue Strat, slamming my foot on distortion pedals,
drowning out Mom's pleas to turn it down
before I pulverize my ear drums.

Through the window, I spotted Dad
outside, bent low among flower beds,
pulling weeds, pausing only for water, never resting
his hardworking hands.

I continued my power chord assault,
never asking if he needed help,
dreaming I'd rock a stage like Cobain,
smash guitars and amps,
make millions to buy new ones.

When Dad came inside, sunburned and tired,
a day's work done,
he paused at my bedroom door, listened to me play
out-of-tune riffs, my attempts to learn
every track on *Nevermind*. He never pounded the door,
never told me to turn it down, never said
I'd need more than a guitar to make it
in this world. He just listened,
then slipped to his room, a quiet fan.

Sunday Dinners

I woke up on Sundays in a slow yawn,
grumbled about the banging of pots and pans,
the loud creak of cupboard doors
as father prepared his homemade pasta sauce.

I drifted downstairs, watched him
stir the sauce slow and steady
with the same wooden spoon,
same white apron splashed red.

I never thanked him
for waking up early every Sunday,
for rolling meatballs in his big palms,
for nursing my groaning stomach.

No sauce tastes the same now,
no matter how many times we read his recipe,
and Sundays no longer mean family dinners,
with all children grown, our father long gone.

Rescuing the Undead

After the shotgun wielding
hero saves the blond,
blasts the final bullet
into the corpse's head,
I'm turned out to night.
She waits for me to stumble home
like one of the undead.

I stagger a few blocks,
remember the nerd who crouched in the cellar,
instead of axing the walking dead,
saving the day and the damsel.

Tired of waiting, I turn around,
pound on the door until she answers.
I climb out of the cellar
until she sees me, kisses me
hard under the pale moon.

Remembering Names

We go around the bonfire circle, fumble names
during our first weekend of freshman year.
We remember more locations and accents—
the drawl of the freckle-faced Southern boy,
the slang of the Brooklyn-based freestyler.

They only name we recall is Mary—
a girl few spoke to
when she slouched in classrooms,
lumbered to her dorm, locked her door,
retreated under covers.
Her classmates never forget her name
after she shot herself.

Now we ask who lives in Ramsey Hall,
if they hear Mary's ghost roll marbles,
flush toilets, slam windows, whisper names
of boys who called her fatso,
laughed at her slow speech, strange accent
during the first weekend of her freshman year.

After we douse the fire,
strum the last acoustic chord,
we speak her name all night,
and will school year to school year.

#27

He yawns away another lecture, dreams
of sinking the game-winning 3, the roar of fans still fresh
in his ears from Friday's game. After class,
he saunters to his dorm, stops to chat to freshman
girls who whisper when he passes, or blush like brides-in-waiting
when he speaks. They call out his number 27,
never his name. He doesn't know
half their names, not even those he kissed or more.
In future games, he'll drain more 3s, excel at fast breaks and layups
before he's tossed out with no degree for missing
class after class. He'll gray and his back will stiffen
like iron as he labors in a warehouse or at Wal-Mart,
trying to remember what he learned before
he flunked out, trying to remember how the crowd
sounded cheering his number, never his name.

Summer at the Press Plant

In the press plant where I worked
at 19, home from college, I befriended Frank,
one pink slip away from eviction, divorce.
We talked horror movies—
Cronenberg's exploding head scenes in *Scanners*,
Romero's classic zombie movies,
Carpenter's remake of *The Thing*.
Frank named every B movie star,
explained the origins of Michael Myers' mask,
or class undertones in *Dawn of the Dead*
better than my tenured film teacher.

Janet, the sharp-tongued worker with black
half-moons under her eyes snapped,
Move it, Frank, whenever he let papers
slip by the assembly line for us to stack
in metal cages. That summer, our faces glowing
with a hard sweat, I survived by talking to Frank,
even when Janet claimed the booze on his breath
made her dizzy. I never believed he slipped out back,
sipped liquor on break, until one morning
he swerved into the parking lot, stumbled into work,
balled his fist on the way out, unemployed again,
red-eyed and worried how to pay rent.

I survived the rest of summer in silence,
counting down days until I returned to campus,
to film classes to share what I learned from Frank.

After Work

he walks the length
of old coal mining streets
under a star-washed dome
after another double shift with no overtime
pay, ears still ringing from the clanging
of factory machines he stood at
until his muscles burned.
His muddy boot kicks the curb outside
the Rusty Nail Bar, where a woman
rejected him away after she noticed
his grease-stained jeans and the smudges
his dirty calloused hands left on beer mugs.
Now he stumbles home and hopes
someone will uncurl his fists as he sleeps.

Morning Routines

The father wakes with crusted eyes
after a night of long, heavy sleep
after yesterday's warehouse shift.
The coffee maker rumbles and beeps like factory machines
while the sun has yet to pierce dark. He dresses,
tiptoes downstairs to feel the furnace for heat
as his wife and kid sleep, then slips out the door
before they wake. He starts his battered Ford,
lips the Springsteen lyric,
It's just the work, the work, the working life.
The sun starts to break
over the horizon and his home,
the sun that will feel so good once he's out of
the windowless warehouse, arms heavy like concrete
from lifting boxes all day, hands sore and blistered, but the sun
so warm against his skin
on the long drive home.

For BP

I saw you last in a heated moment, fists clenched,
our faces a few inches apart, red from whiskey
and heated insults we hurled at each other
after years of friendship. You called me yuppie
for finishing college, then grad school, while you
drifted from factories to call centers,
smart enough to attend college, but never
given the chance because of an absent father, low funds,
a system that requires money and connections for admittance.
We would have pummeled each other over class division
and education if our friend Mike didn't lower our fists,
push us to separate rooms where we cooled off
until I kicked you out. Then I wondered
how it could have been if our places
had been switched, if you had school while I swept
factory floors, if I would have balled my fists and wanted to brawl
over unequal opportunity, if you had the 3-room pad and parties
while I walked home in summer rain, fists buried in my pockets.

Before He Enlisted

I used to believe a thousand protest signs
could alter decisions of lawmakers and kings,
save my friend from eight more months in Iraq.
Now his baby boy wails at home,
and his wife waits,
hugs his pillow to her chest,
or clenches his T-shirt, pretends he's close.

I used to believe in the power
of a few chords, distorted, blaring
from vibrating speakers. My friend fronted
the band, roared a cover
of the Dead Kennedys' track
"Stars and Stripes of Corruption."
Months later, he enlisted.
Now his guitar sits in cases,
locked in storage until his return.

I used to believe in mapped out
plans made with him—
dorm room arrangements,
blocks of study time, then parties
after our classes at Temple, West Chester, or Drexel.

Now I cling to his wife's words—
He'll be back, he'll come home soon.
I wait for our once-a-month Skype chat
when he says, *After this, I'm enrolling in school.*
I give him a thumbs-up, believe in
the grainy webcam video,
the microphoned voice that tells me
he's still alive.

Upon Hearing the News More Post Offices to Close

I think of our town's lone mail clerk,
all the orders he ships,
boxes he seals,
envelopes he stuffs in drab back rooms
after the counter closes.
He receives few thank-yous
from impatient lawyers on lunch breaks,
parents with less minutes to spare,
college kids picking up care packages. His hands
never tire, doling out stamps, swiping debit cards as dim light
shines on his graying hair.
Some huff and stamp out if the line
snakes around corners, but still he smiles, calls the next
customer to the counter. Above him hangs a mural of railroad
workers with pained faces, laying track for railways that used to
ship letters coast to coast years before our clerk
labored alone, keeping the line and mail trucks moving.

Muse

She'll wake to the sound of a cork
twisted free from a bottle,
steal your last smoke,
pry you away from back walls,
pull you to the dance floor.

She'll kiss on a first date,
strip down to black panties, a bra
after you've left. You need
better lines before she beckons you
inside to touch her skin,
feel her body against yours.

She'll leave you red-eyed,
waiting for a returned text.
You thought she's the type
who lingers by the phone.
She'll call if she wants to call.
Then you'll know you've earned another date.

Gypsy

My gaze caught her long ruffled dress,
sequins that shined under streetlights,
purple heels that imprinted fresh snow,
bracelets that jangled on her wrists all night.

She stopped roaming from guest to guest
after I took her hand, led her
to the couch, as people passed in waves
and hip-hop beats grew mute as our ears
absorbed each other's words only.

Back at my place, she shivered and said,
Soon I'm gonna roam again,
hop a train to Chicago or Cali.
I wanted her to stay as we lit a fire,
talked in silent voices.

When I woke, I found her note,
Sorry, babe. I'm going back home.
Through the window, I watched soft lumps of snow
cover her fleeting footsteps.

How I Remember Her

I keep her red-haired in my mind,
with a disarming smile, a fistful of workers' rights leaflets.
She is not yet a young mother
weighed down by baby bottle bags,
pushing a stroller past the courthouse
where she stood many mornings to protest
unfair government wages and reduced union rights.

I keep her in my mind wearing hand-sewn patches—
a fist holding grain,
Food Not Bombs stitched under the logo.
She is not yet an office worker,
drifting from temp job to temp job,
bound to a desk, eyes fixed on a screen,
fingers locked to computer keys.

I keep her in my mind granddaughter of a Quaker
pacifist who taught us
don't sneer or bite back if labeled
pinkos, hippies, liberal pussies by counter-protesters.
She is not yet the wife of a factory worker
whose knuckles are scraped and bruised,
who stumbles to bed, too drunk to please his wife.

I keep her in my mind on the porch swing,
moments before she told me she's pregnant
by a man she loves sometimes, when he's nice,
that she'll have to quit college, take care of the kid,
that she'll raise him to follow the same ethics
she preached many mornings
I joined her at courthouse protests.

Work Clothes

His sleeves, short and tight
against his gym-toned arms, biceps inked
with two tattoos, the left the date
he shipped to Iraq, the right the date he returned.

His shirt, faded blue with an oil and grease stink,
buttons barely able to contain his chest,
puffed out when he talks politics,
or scans bleeding headlines about car bombs,
another hometown soldier dead.

His leather wallet, stuffed with two crumbled twenties,
a picture of a chipped-tooth Iraqi boy,
smiling after American soldiers made peace
with fistfuls of candy.

His boots, as black as desert night skies,
scuffed at the tips from all the times he kicked the wall
after another hood swallowed his wrench.

His collar, stiff and tight as he crawls under cars,
then sweats and thinks of all the job applications he filed,
all the times he signed his name and hoped
this one would earn him an interview.

According to a report released by the Bureau of Labor Statistics, the unemployment rate for veterans who served on active duty in the U.S. Armed Forces at any time since September 2001—a group referred to as Gulf War-era II veterans—was 12.1% in 2011, higher than the national average, but for veterans age 18-24, the unemployment rate was 29.1%.

A Mother's Concern

When the mother retreats to the break room,
away from badgering customers at one job,
impatient diners at another,
she wonders what kids say
about her son, the lunch he packs daily—
white bread, apples from ALDI that brown
in hours, stale crackers, thin slices of cheese,
all food stamps can afford.
He wants what other kids have, a chance
to stand in line at lunch for ice cream,
even an orange that glows in the hands of other boys
like fire, but mother's double shifts
leave little after bills.
When he comes home, silent about a boy who knocked
his imitation Air Jordans or no-name shirt,
she knows his anger by the way he digs
his fingernails into his palms, or retreats
to his room to read and ignore his stomach groans.
She wishes to hold him, rock him
like when he was a giggling baby boy
and she said, *We'll be just fine.*
Now he shrugs her off, plugs his ears
with headphones. She clings to the hope
he'll never know what it's like
to raise a son who stares across the table and asks,
Can't we eat out just once?
She never wants him to know
searing blisters, throbbing headaches from working doubles.
She imagines him behind a desk, hot shot CEO,
first in family to finish college,
or a teacher, confident in a classroom,
willing to lend extra dollars to all the students

Lone Protestor

Nothing is coming down the street,
no mass of protestors, no movement,
no politicians to read the ex-teacher's rain-soaked sign.
She is as common to them as daily constituent calls.
Still, she shows up, flashes her red letters on soggy cardboard,
Jobs, not cuts. She counts
the number of days since she first filed
unemployment claims, barely remembering
what it's like to occupy
a classroom with the knowledge and power
she had as a middle school teacher.
Now she stands on the corner with her sign, while some
mistake her for the homeless woman
who roams downtown, chain smoking,
muttering to anyone who will listen.

One Night

She parked her pink Corvette curbside outside the hotel,
ran her fingers through her black wind-whipped hair,
touched up her cherry-red lipstick.
I bought her a drink
before she reached the bar,
fell in love
before we even talked.

She traced her black fingernails
along the martini glass, licked her lips and said,
Boy, I need a man who makes the devil pale.

She caught the guy with spider web tattoos
who tossed back whiskey shots,
howled, cracked pool balls.
Her low-cut cocktail dress could ensnare
any guy who looked her way.
I listened to her heels click clack
as she exited the bar,
his inked arm around her shoulder.

Now I hook my fingers around a six-pack,
drain each beer as I hear
moaning through the hotel's cheap walls,
and wonder if it's her.
I crush the last can, fall asleep,
wake up with the faded smear,
her lipstick on my left cheek.

How She Hides Her Age

She still dyes her hair Smurf blue,
years later, after our first show
at Cafe Roach, where she leaned against the brick wall,
inched up her safety-pinned skirt,
flashed her first circle pit scars.
Her body was a blank canvas then,
free of tattoo sleeves and piercings.

She is the last of our crew like this.
Mohawk Tony moved to Manhattan,
cut his hair for corporate.
Rock Girl Cindy runs a woman's center,
pulls in a university salary.
I teach literature to yawning youth,
high school students that snicker when I say,
I saw the Ramones twice,
broke my wrist in the pit.
Yeah, sure, Teach, they say.

They'd believe my blue-haired friend,
who punches her own record store clock.
They won't see the age lines near her eyes,
hidden by big black shades,
or streaks of gray in her hair,
covered by fresh hair dye.
She still practices her cool years later,
her body an inked and tattooed canvas now.

The Plot

He says, *honey, let's go,* and she follows to Fred's,
the High Street bar where men bark at TVs like Romans
seated before a bread and circus show, howling and drooling
at blood sports. She sips her martini, then circles the rim
with her red fingernail while her husband sucks down shots
like a man 20 years younger, pounding the table for more.
She wonders if Roman women followed to stadiums or stayed home
scrubbing floors, and which was worse. She has been his habit for 10 years,
10 years he came home with booze breath.
She plots how best to leave him,
maybe slip a note under his pillow, or shout and stomp out,
though dressed in cymbals, leaving him to cook with clumsy
hands, to flip through recipes and beg
for an easy meal because she learned
there is more to life than this.

Old Lovers

He answered her motel call for company,
pulled her close, wrapped her in his long arms,
the same arms she used to imagine
caressing when she watched him swing bats
at their high school ball field.

For two hours, she made up for months
she ached to be touched,
nights she pulled a pillow close,
pretended she could feel his facial stubble prick her cheeks.

The old lovers finished, sparked cigarettes,
sat on the deck. They knew that come daybreak
they'd gather their clothes,
bathe and leave because she had her New York job,
and he his hometown carpenter work.

He liked to remember how his name rolled from her tongue,
and she the strength of his hands
tracing her curves in the dark.
They always left before sunlight revealed
growing streaks of gray in their hair,
fine lines near their eyes,
bodies tired and sore, in need of rest
before meeting again.

Ride Home, Rutgers, November

Bob Dylan rasps
        on my car radio—
            Days are gettin' short.
    Night comes in a'fallin'.
His dustbowl growl
           reminds me of cool
autumn nights we plucked LPs
        from milk crates,
              listened
to the scratch of the needle against wax.

Now I drive
      home
          from her place
    alone,
          under the wafer of moon,
      this grumpy November sky.
I crank the volume,
            recall her words—
     We should see other people—
            and how I looked away,
focused
      on the fat Oak tree center campus,
         its last few leaves
           clinging
      against the pull and push of winds
      as forceful
         as bursts of harmonica blues blasting
      through my car's stereo,
bringing me back to nights
        at her apartment,
listening to Dylan snarl
        over acoustic chords.

What Remains

I pull out her silver necklace
cough from the dust of old days,
try to find traces of lingering
perfume she bought that day in Brooklyn
when I had time off to visit.

I paid for cab after cab that day
because she said she hates the sound of rain,
and I remembered our nights together,
how she couldn't sleep if rain
drummed on our roof,
pinged against garbage cans.
Sounds like ghosts
tapping at windows, the past
always whispering, she'd say.
When I asked what ghosts,
or brushed her back or breasts,
she recoiled under covers.

After cab rides, we found her favorite cafe
where we had our first date five years ago,
same crank umbrellas, same cannoli, same espresso shots.
Then I had to leave, back to the West Coast,
out of money, out of time.

Now I raise her jewelry to my lips,
cough from the dust of old ghosts.

In Back of the Club

We drive home from Philly, our hair matted,
shirts sticky, reeking of sweat from the sweltering club
where we watched Hot Water Music's reunion set.
Clusters of tattooed fans drained PBRs,
crowd surfed, jerked their bodies
against each other, raised their fists
to front man Chuck Ragan's guttural rasp,
backed by ear-bruising drum beats,
paper-cutting bass rhythm. We cemented ourselves
in back of the club, earplugs in, too timid
to inch up front. We remembered
how we used to thrash in the pit, fearless
of muscle aches and purple bruises.
Now we're the guys we used to mock,
aging, arm-crossed hipsters who remember what it's like
to know every track, to sing until hoarse.
Now I strain my eyesight on the drive home,
nearly lulled to sleep by white highway dashes that pass
as quickly as fleeting youth.

Reunion

After I moved back home to teach,
my old friend told me
she lived in trees for two months to fight
deforestation in Oregon.
I wanted to raise an eyebrow, ask,
Why you still doing this?
Instead, I sipped my latte,
nodded like an interested consumer, asked,
How'd you get there? How'd you survive?
Train-hopping, and on nuts and berries, she said.

She was still the same girl from high school
in scuffed Docs, hand-sewn Crass patches, the wide-eyed activist
who sat outside Cafe Roach, puffed
a smoke, quoted Emma Goldman—
If I can't dance to it, it's not my revolution.

After our reunion, I saw her
weeks later, the red washed out
of her hair. She told me
her father died and she didn't care about
tired old scenes, boring four-chord music.
I told her about my dad, how he could only speak
in moans and slurred words after the stroke
weeks before he died.

She squeezed my hand, followed me
back to my place, blared a Clash record from storage.
She bobbed her head, lipped lyrics
to "Janie Jones," remembering how she
slammed against bodies in the pit,
sweaty and bruised, turned out to night
with fresh circle pit scars.

Old Friend

Friends say she's unfit to sit near.
They tell me she prowls clubs,
buys shots for young men,
sinks her nails into their hips and backs
until their skin purples and sores.

They tell me she disguises her age,
covers wrinkles with concealer,
reddens her hair on weeknights,
practices pick-up lines in public bathrooms.

When friends ask what she is to me,
I shrug, say a good friend,
someone I talk to until 2 am
about Keats' rhythms or the war in Iraq.

When I ask them if they've ever seen her
dab foundation to cover up lines,
or buy drinks for young guys at bars,
they shove their hands in their pockets,
mumble about rumors and misunderstandings.

Then I grin when she walks in—
black cocktail dress, red heels that click clack
to a bar stool she steals from friends
to sit near me all night.

Saturday Soul Singer

Her face pains agains the mike,
pulled back as she releases, wails
a long note, backed by trumpet,
bursts of sax, steady bass.

After she holds the note, finishes,
her lips curve into a smile.
She tugs at her blue velvet dress,
steps off stage in stilettos,
away from white lights that shined on her fine black skin.

White men in iron-pressed khakis
puff their cigars, smile
next to clapping wives who've never heard
Miles moan what it's like to be blue,
or Billie's burned voice against sleek piano.
They'll go home humming a few bars.

Natural Cool

She found me in a crowd of fifty
indie rockers crossing their arms,
trying not to care, not to dance to discordant
chords shaking the cafe's wooden walls.

We weaved our way to a cozy corner
where I watched her black skirt sway
like ocean waves as she danced to the burst
of power chords, unconcerned
with the rigid rules of hipster cool.

Post-set, I paced the sidewalk,
buried my shaky hands in pockets,
waited for her to finish with friends,
to give me her number, to ask for mine.

Post-show, I thought about
her green ocean eyes and natural cool,
how she broke from wallflowers
as immutable as statues,
swayed, cheered, clapped to every song,
then gave me her number, knowing
I'd have the guts to call.

Stranded and Staying

Rafted and tangled in sheets,
eyes aflutter, he doesn't want to leave
her Calypso island, or check his watch
on her dresser, jeweled and decanted with her smell.

Upstairs, the neighbor's puppy
scurries across the floor, his beagle yelp heard below.
Outside, children chatter on sidewalks,
until the bus brakes squeal and the door opens.

He hears all this, knows he must iron his clothes,
ready for work, but he stays stranded,
if only for a moment, resting his head on her chest,
counting her heartbeats and breath.

Storm Coming

We wait and watch the gray mass
creep in like that scene in *Poltergeist*
when storm clouds loom over the family home
just before the crack of thunder and TV static.
The night we watched the film,
you clenched my arm, but said, *It's just a movie.*

Now we cling to each other, waiting,
wondering what this storm will chew up, spit out,
how rain and wind will sound slicing
through shingles, heaving against houses,
how many trees will shatter windshields,
crash power lines, blacken laptops and TVs.

When it's over, we'll inspect the car,
drive through neighborhoods, eye downed lines,
broken branches. You'll loosen your grip on my arm,
as you did when the horror movie ended, and say,
It was just a storm.

Listening to the Neighbors

The wife next door shrieks at her husband,
her voice shrill enough to jolt us from sleep
as we press our ears to paper walls,
attentive like boxing fans waiting for the final blow,
a KO. I imagine her face fire red, one fist
clenched as she smacks her palm again and again to prove
each point. We hear little from him,
who I picture crouched in a corner,
like a fighter trying to withstand blow after blow,
her verbal insults and frequent fuck-yous,
though she means to banish him from their home,
away from their unborn boy.
You hold me tight, both of us glad
our tongues are not daggers as we hear
her muffled cries, once their curses cease and they realize
how much their words bloodied each other round after round,
how hard it is to revive love
after counting it out.

Evacuation

The governor and mayor, men safe in mansions,
pushed the evacuation notice to noon,
while my car inched towards home,
closer to National Guard tanks and flood zones,
where vans and pick-ups cut across side streets,
loaded with as much as a family could save
stuffed within four doors, the rest roof-strapped.
I pounded the wheel, cursed my decision to work
that morning, thinking the rain would ease, until I saw
I-81 resemble a doomsday movie—
rivers of cars honking horns, while the Susquehanna swelled.

Once home, I hugged you hard,
and like thieves, we ransacked our apartment,
pouring books, clothes, jewelry into boxes,
then raised furniture on milk crates,
while we whispered, *the levees will hold, the levees will hold*.
We shut all doors, locked all windows, feared
returning to warped floors, mud-caked walls.
We fled with what we could, whispered again,
the levees will hold.

For four days, we watched constant coverage—
homes swept from streets in Tunkhannock,
pushed downstream, smashed into bridges,
cars swallowed, towns without levees devoured.
Near our home, the river heaved against the dike,
fizzling and bubbling against white barriers
like soda leaking through a punctured can.

When we heard the order to return home,
the sun poked through clouds, first time
in days. This time, no tombstones or caskets
floated down the road from the Forty Fort Cemetery
like in '72. This time, our town's streets stayed dry,
homes as they had been left.

Months later, we biked along the dike,
gazed at chairs and clothes floating downstream,
a mud-slimed refrigerator caught in a tree,
others' misfortunes swallowed and spit out at the river's edge.

*In September of 2011, major rainfall caused by Tropical Storm Lee led
to the evacuation of several communities along the Susquehanna River.
In Wilkes-Barre, PA, 65,000 people were evacuated, and another 35,000
people were evacuated in surrounding counties, according to Reuters.
The flooding conjured memories of the devastation caused by Hurricane
Agnes in 1972.*

After Working Hours

She comes home to a husband
just as bone-tired, slow to the kitchen
for a snack before sleep.

In dreams, she sees her hair streaked gray,
her back hunched from years behind a counter.
She still hears her manager's screeching voice
call for clean-up in aisle 9.

Her husband also dreams work sounds—
buzzsaws grinding down wood, hammers pounding nails,
the site boss bellowing, *Move your ass, boys!*

When they wake, they speak nothing
of his blistered fingers and swollen knuckles,
her headaches caused by nagging customers.
He pours her coffee with two scoops of sugar,

his demeanor as pleasant as a well-tipped waiter's.
She picks up the paper, then slips her hand over his,
feeling warmth beneath his callouses and cracked skin.

The Old Neighborhood

When I return to the old neighborhood,
my Italian neighbor says it's *finito.*
Look at the yards cluttered with junk cars,
wooden fences cracked, kicked in,
battered doors hanging from hinges, she says.
I see shirtless children racing through sprinklers,
backyards cramped with barbeque pits and lawn chairs.
If I say we all need
somewhere to live, somewhere affordable
she hisses, *I'm just speaking my mind.*

When I gaze out her window
at leaves falling on Diamond Field
where I played ball as a child, I see
black and brown boys banking free throws
off backboards, dunking on netless hoops.
I hear children laughing, dashing down
slides, rushing from first base to home.

Empty Intermediate School

It sits atop Providence Hill,
windows boarded or cracked,
doorknobs rusted and locked,
sidewalks and stairwells vine-strangled
and blocked. Hallways used to bustle
with students scurrying to class,
locker doors swinging open and shut,
teachers lecturing that children can be
anything they want to be, until factories closed
and parents found pink slips. Grown, the kids fled
their rust belt state, found promise in Philly, or jobs
in New York. Now remaining workers search
classifieds, cut out ad after ad,
drift from job to job,
finding whatever they can to get by
like scrappy alley cats left to roam
the school's empty hallways,
catching mice and rats to survive.

Brian Fanelli

Outside Tent Cities

We drove two hours, marveled at hundreds of tents
circling Philly's City Hall and signs that read,
$40,000 in debt, no job.
Two tours in Iraq, home now, no job.
Two degrees, underemployed at Walgreens.
Sunlight cleared the hazy morning and we broke
into committees, vowed to occupy
banks, bridges, schools, subways,
to march and chant,
feed the forgotten homeless.

Later, blocks away, a homeless man
caught us in the crosshairs of his gaze,
his eyes black like the scarf
wrapped around his scarred face.
We stuffed our hands in pockets, walked on
like tourists, even as he extended his palm,
rattled his change cup.
Then we ate in the makeshift kitchen
of the tent city, taking bites
of donated bread before we drove back home,
bodies full, but haunted by a heavy weight—
the homeless man's stare,
blisters on his brown palms—
the only sign he needs.

Mr. Scranton

He speaks in a dustbowl growl like Dylan,
rolls up his sleeves like Woody Guthrie,
has hands as calloused as a guitar player's fingertips.
He's part Italian, part Irish, part Polish,
a mechanic, carpenter, warehouse worker,
40-hour-per-week union man.
He drives to dive bars in a dinged-up
Ford that backfires and booms like shotgun rounds.
He wakes for Sunday mass,
scrubs his palms caked with dirt,
grease layered under his fingernails.
He cooks Sunday dinners with his wife—
plates full of pasta and meatballs.
He walks rusted train tracks, remembers
whistles in the distance, his father
who hammered railroad spikes, his grandfathers
who labored in mines.
He smudges newspaper ink at the Glider Diner,
sips 99 cent coffee, remembers
penny candy stores, $1 movie theaters,
now storefronts as empty as abandoned mine shafts.

Advice From Grandfather

I want to meet my grandfather,
hear his smoke gravel voice, feel
his hands, hardened
and cracked from 12-hour mine shifts,
show him a picture of me
with ice cream-painted lips,
the boy he never met.
I want to ask him
how his generation survived
hunger pains, low-wage jobs, a world war,
what advice he'd give
a generation in debt,
stuck in a great recession.
You too will survive, he'd say.
I want to pop open his beers,
watch him take long, hard swigs,
I'd thank him for his time and labor,
for loving his wife, tending to his kids,
for waking up early, dressing in blue-black cold
just to survive.
I'd look at his palms, swollen and steeled, soot
crusted under his fingernails and know
my generation will also survive.

Snapshot of My Attic

I still have Star Wars figures ziplocked
in drawers from days I imagined myself
Luke Skywalker clashing light sabers with Vader,
or Han Solo, pointing his laser gun at Jabba's fat belly
telling him, *Get lost, punk.*

I still have the chipped Harmony Sunburst,
purchased by Dad at the Steamtown Trading Post.
It sits in a dusty case now, its strings mute next to
a 100-watt amp that shook my bedroom walls
when I ditched high school dances,
riffed hours away instead.

I still have these boxes labeled and marked
because one day I may have a son
who will curl his hand around
action figures, pretend he's piloting
the Millennium Falcon through space,
a son may grow up to ignite the fretboard
with red hot riffs until his fingers ache,
a son who could ask me to buy him guitars and amps
that will vibrate his bedroom walls
as his old man tries to sleep. I will still
show him a riff or two if asked,
Play it again, Pop. Teach me what you know.

Public Displays

He jerked and blushed when she kissed him
hard at the red light on 5th,
next to a brown-haired businessman
too busy checking texts to notice.
See, no one cares, she said.
He groaned, turned away,

until she pinched his bottom. Red-eared,
purple-faced, he froze.
Damn it! Not here, not now, he said.
She grinned, squeezed his hand,
cupped his chin, leaned in.

His heart thudded so hard
he thought it'd crack his ribcage.
Come on. Kiss me, she said,
squeezing his hand harder
until he leaned over on the NYC street,
kissed her puckered lips.
She smiled, eased her grip,
walked forward with him on green.

For a Moment

Damn, teach got game, says Miguel,
who high fives other students in class
after I tell them my girlfriend
quit eating meat for me. This follows
one of their essays about hunting, a cousin
who loaded a rifle with hollow point
bullets to shoot rabbits, leaving nothing
but twitching bodies, crimson drops in snow,
leaving students to groan in reaction to the writing,
the pop, pop, pop of gunfire.
We drift away from narrative writing after my confession.
I become human to them, more than a droning stiff
in iron-pressed khakis and Polos, more than
a lecturer who relies on PowerPoint like a teleprompter,
sometimes stumbling over lines. We laugh,
if just for a moment, at Miguel's joke
that I got game.

The Married and Single Men

I.

The spent father envies his single cousin,
whose arms weren't weighed down
by three baby bags, two strollers, a bottle
when he entered the family party.

The father wants one night alone
to kick off his shoes, crank the big screen TV's volume,
lounge on the couch, watch every baseball play
without answering the baby's all-night calls,
or worrying about snow heaving against doors,
the furnace coughing and wheezing like a black lung.

II.

The single cousin envies the new father,
who feeds his son a bottle,
draws crowds at the party with his wife.
The cousin wonders what it's like to feel
a newborn's hands curl around his finger.

For years he scribbled his number on bar napkins,
yet never copied his apartment key for anyone,
or invited a woman back after one night.
Every dinner now he sits alone,
across from an empty chair, wondering
what lines would make a woman stay.

Missed Cues

She drags her fork across the plate,
pokes at peas until he asks,
What's wrong now?

He pounds a basketball on blacktop,
curses bricked free throws and missed 3s,
until she stands on the porch, hands on hips and asks,
Coming inside yet?

She cranks the oldies station,
screams along to "A Hard Day's Night"
after last night's spat over her in-laws' visit.

He slouches on the couch, loosens his tie,
drains a beer as she channel surfs,
waiting for a hello or kiss,
more than his half sighs.

They wake up before work, mumble good morning
like two strangers on a subway,
waiting for the next stop, for the other exit
so the one who stays has more room.

When She Left

The sky was a deep headstrong blue
the day she left. Leaves crunched under her
fleeting footsteps as I watched
her hail a cab back to her place.

Inside, I touched what belonged to her—
red heels she left when she stormed out,
dog-eared books with margin notes,
the chipped yellow mug she used many mornings.

Sometimes I wait, watch through the window
for the cab to pull up,
for both of us to say sorry,
for her dusty possessions to have use again.

When she doesn't come, I listen to the TV for company
as sunlight pours through living room windows,
the sky the same headstrong blue
as the day she left.

To Forget

His weathered hand reaches for the high shelf,
calls another bottle of rum to forget
wind-blown January days, the raw,
cold silence of his apartment, the impending tomorrows
repetitive from his daily factory grind.

His lips curve into a grin
after another swig to forget gray
workplace walls, the hard cement floor,
the hungry machines he feeds for 8 hours,
shifting from one foot to another.

He blares the TV, cheers
his Bulls without a woman to hush
turn it down. He pictures himself in the game,
driving to the hoop, cutting through defensive screens,
dishing assists, dropping points like Derrick Rose.

He imagines #1 stitched into his jersey
like his high school days, his legs sturdy and strong back then
to shoot jumpers, sink 3s, his name flashed on posters
in big, bold letters, years before his muscles throbbed at work,
shifting from one foot to another in a sad slouch.

Winter Break-up

Thoughts slushed in his mind like snow or sleet,
he opens his mouth and words fall
like anvils. His ex backs up, waiting
for a better apology, for something poetic to fly
from his mouth like birds to convince her to stay,
to justify nights he stumbled home and slurred excuses.
February and the sadness of early evening hits him
as he remembers their first few nights together,
snow drifts piling outside, the couple's low, joyous cries
a memory now because nothing flares up in her anymore,
no matter how sweet his kiss or caress.

After Argument

Her skin damp from the shower,
she makes love to him in the morning,
after last night's fight over cold pasta fagioli,
when he said, *We've had better dinners,*
and she cried, *I try, God damn, I try,*
then clenched her purse, stormed to the door,
until he pulled her close,
disarmed her with a kiss.

Now they cling to each other's moorings,
ache for each other's touch like adolescent lovers
just finished with a first kiss. She rests her head
on his chest, listens to his familiar breathing
as a new day begins.

Escape

The word nuke populates headlines again,
this time Iran, while in Syria
tanks crawl through streets. Blood darkens
porch stoops. Here, senators and congressmen
puff out their chests, finger point and push
for more decade-long wars. Gas prices surge
higher than Katrina's aftermath and a decade
punctuated by Iraq and Afghanistan. I grab your hand
after a sunshower baptizes our street. We inhale
the steaming scent of wet cement. I want to run
through city streets with you, cut across town,
away from cable news cranked in living rooms and headlines
wailing in the wind, pulsating with potential war and violent
uprising in another country where a girl grabs the hand
of a boy to run over rubble.

On the Highway Home

Long branches stick out, narrow and dull,
as you drive along the highway,
praying for overbearing winter to end.
You think of your kid, your wife
at home, if they shoveled
the sidewalk, if the remaining car
is buried beneath mounds of white.
Your chest tightens as you remember
the low amount of milk in the fridge,
the few slices of bread left.
You think of the basement furnace
that chokes like a smoker's lung,
the cold that pushes against the house.
You remember Frost's poem "Storm Fear,"
the raw winds that squelched the cabin fire,
the family of three trapped inside, their safety
so distant. You think of night, so cold and heavy, and count
the hours until you're home,
safe, back from the business trip. You wonder
how you'll drive over black ice, through pelts of hail,
how you'll survive, knuckles white on the wheel.

At 18

He marched through February sleet and snow,
shuffled through protest cages like cattle, billy clubbed
by Philly PD, months before bombs
pummeled Baghdad, before his sign's red ink smeared
and looked like blood dripping on his black boots.

He defrosted his numb cheeks and ice-gnawed hands
over hot cocoa in a cafe where June Bugg,
his activist lover who smelled like autumn,
designed DIY flyers stamped with Howard Zinn's words—
War is the enemy of humanity.

At open mics, he signed his name Peaceful Pete,
rasped Dylan covers over his out-of-tune Epiphone,
backed by June Bugg's tambourine chimes.
After 3-song sets, they sparked cigarettes that burned
like coals against the night sky.

A decade later June Bugg married a banker,
slips to South Street bookstores now,
has an affair with lefty literature in aisles
where her husband won't catch her
reciting lines by Adrienne Rich and Muriel Rukeyser.

A decade later, he teaches history to youth that yawn
when he mentions Zinn or Chomsky, but he still lectures
and trusts one of them will pick up *A People's History,*
enroll in an activist army, raise a picket sign,
join him on the streets against the next war.

Another Election

No matter which channel he changed,
more tallies, more defeats,
big screen TVs bleeding red.
He sighed, sunk on the couch.

So, did our guy win? his wife asked.
Mad enough to spit, he bit his lip,
mumbled, *The country's swung to the right,
from Texas to Colorado.*

She shrugged, said, *It'll shift again.
How do you feel about a new table set?*
Shaking his head, he cranked the volume,
cursed the flashing Rs falling into victory columns.

What do you think? she asked, nudging him.
*There's always another election. We need a new table set.
Remember how you pouted for days
after Reagan won, then Bush I and II?*
I never pouted, he said.

She smiled as he tried
to stay sullen and sober.
She nudged him until he cracked,
and they laughed, giddy long into the night,
even if she mentioned the table set,
or the pundits prattled about politics.

The Stroke

It was like death blew open the door,
stormed to the father's room, squeezed his hand
until he fell to the floor.
Then death yanked him up, punched him in the mouth
with the strength of 100 schoolyard bullies
until he no longer formed words. But he didn't
collapse again or die, just tried
to roll Rs on his tongue,
to call for his wife and son,
then answer them in long, painful moans
of a broken tongue.

Speaking From a Sick Bed

I feel my son squeeze my hand,
half hear him say,
I'll make it, Pop,
graduate, build front-page bylines,
cut out every article for you.
After another morphine shot,
his words fade to me,
like a broken radio station,
or smeared newspaper ink.

I called for him at night,
wanted him right here
to squeeze his hand,
let him know I'm still here,
like his first day of school
when he gripped my hand down the hallway.

I want to rise from bed, say, *Son,*
I'm not going anywhere,
but my tongue is dry
my speech slowed from the first stroke.
I speak now in moans,
a squeeze of the hand that says,
I'm still here.

Possessions

White-knuckled, she clenches
                  the Old Spice bottle,
      squirts the cologne
          twice,
remembers
      his body reflected in the mirror—
              face shaved after a shower,
clothes folded
        neatly on the bed,
ready to be pulled over
               his long arms and legs
that were still strong enough
        to pick her up.

      She sets the cologne aside,
           folds his mechanic shirt,
      lays it across the bed,
            kisses
        the collar and cloth she scrubbed
until her hands pruned and grease stains were removed.

Sometimes she buttoned up
          his work shirt,
kissed his neck
        as he laced
        his black work boots
that still sit by the door,
        polished, though ready
for his return.

After

After the loss, she scrubs
bathroom floors, kitchen sinks
until her hands ache and she forgets
the sound of water running
in the early a.m. before her husband
used to leave for work.

After the loss, she lounges
on the leather chair, flips through pages
of paperbacks, or channel surfs until time
marches past midnight, and she dozes off
without sleeping in her bed
too big for one.

After the loss, she wakes
with a stiff neck, sore back,
a long sigh as she opens
the curtains, squints in daylight.
She works longer than the normal 9-5,
busies her mind by typing reports to delay
long evenings at home, listening
to walls creak, and eating dinner alone
across from an empty chair.

Now on Sunday mornings she chops
onions, peppers, carrots, until her hands and body
tire, but she has enough food for family
dinners when she can finally smile and see
all children and grandchildren seated,
together again, remembering Pop.

After School Drives

Father's gray Ford sat curbside after school,
Elvis CDs turned low because he knew I disliked
the King, preferred Johnny Cash, who he sometimes played,
dropping his voice low to mimic the man-in-black's
steady-like-a-freight-train vocals. If he sang
loudly, windows rolled down on a spring day,
I slouched in the seat, worried
someone may have seen me sitting shotgun
with the out-of-tune driver. When he didn't sing,
he asked me about girls, guitar lessons
baseball tryouts. I gave curt responses,
half-sentence replies like any teen
concerned with being cool, even though father
picked me up daily, saved me
from the crowded bus, two-hour
countryside drives, made longer
in winter. Years later, after father passed,
I missed those after school drives, the chance
to fill silence with conversation, even those moments
he crooned so off-key even I had to laugh.

Where Poetry Exists

I tell my students poetry is found
in empty mine shafts that run under
their old town, that it exists
in the history within jagged rock walls,
dirt that streaked miners' faces,
dust that caked their boots.
I tell them poetry is found
in the lines of their great-grandfather's hands,
scarred from toiling in the town's black underbelly.
I tell them poetry is found
in conversations construction workers have
at diners, that it exists in the details
of what they say, how they say it.
I tell them poetry is found
in the kiss between a husband and wife, home
from a 10-hour shift, and their long sigh
after they collapse on the couch.
I tell them poetry is found in labor
of men and women who still populate
their hometown, that to write it seriously
should be as habitual as waking
to the alarm clock's buzz and meeting the work day.

BRIAN FANELLI lives in Pennsylvania and teaches English at Lackawanna College in Scranton. His poetry has been nominated for a Pushcart Prize and has been published by *Chiron Review, Boston*

 *Literary Magazine, Word Riot, Red Rock Review, The Portland Review, Pennsylvania Literary Journal, Harpur Palate, San Pedro River Review, vox poetica, Third Wednesday, Solstice Literary Magazine, Evening Street Review*, and other journals on line and in print. He is the author of the chapbook *Front Man* (Big Table Publishing), and his reviews and essays have been published by *PANK* and *Poets' Quarterly*. Brian holds an MFA from Wilkes University and is completing his PhD at SUNY Binghamton. For more information and to read his blog, visit www.brianfanelli.com.

Acknowledgments

Thank you to my family and friends for their continued support, and thank you to the various art venues, bookstores, and coffee shops that have hosted me for readings and workshops over the last few years. I am also grateful to the Wilkes University MFA community and to Annmarie Lockhart and her staff at Unbound Content.

Special thanks to Jenna for her continued love and support, as well as her critical eye and intelligence.

Publication Credits

Special acknowledgment is made to the following publications in which some of these poems first appeared, sometimes in different forms:

Blue Lotus Review: "Lone Protestor," "Summer at the Press Plant"
Boston Literary Magazine: "After Working Hours"
Eunoia Review: "Listening to the Neighbors"
Evening Street Review: "How I Remember Her"
Foliate Oak: "At 18"
Harpur Palate: "After Work"
Indigo Rising Magazine: "Muse," "Rescuing the Undead," "Old Lovers," "The Old Neighborhood," "What Remains"
Pennsylvania Literary Journal: "One Night"
The Portland Review: "Missed Cues"
Red Rock Review: "The Stroke," "Storm Coming"
San Pedro River Review: "How She Hides Her Age"
Solstice Literary Magazine: "Before He Enlisted"
vox poetica: "The Plot," "Where Poetry Exists"
Word Fountain: "Evacuation," "Ride Home, Rutgers, November," "Saturday Soul Singer," "On the Highway Home"
WritingRaw.com: "Old Friend," "Gypsy"
Young American Poets: "Dive"
Yes, Poetry: "Remembering Names"

The poems "To Forget," "For BP," "Upon Hearing News More Post Offices to Close," "Sunday Dinners," "After School Drives," "Mr. Scranton," and "A Mother's Concern," along with an introduction about the poems, first appeared in the summer 2012 issue of *Third Wednesday*.

Praise for *All That Remains:*

From regret about time squandered and words not spoken to impressing some girl at the pool with a perfect dive, every emotion in the spectrum is plucked by master storyteller Brian Fanelli in his new book, *All That Remains.* As with all good comings of age, disasters unfold, people age, become disenchanted, and watch loved ones die, but here too you will find the pure beauty of existence and the triumph of the human spirit. For years Fanelli has been a favorite at *Boston Literary Magazine. All That Remains* is why.

—Robin Stratton, editor, *Boston Literary Magazine*

What remains? Memories that haunt. The lingering presence of loved ones lost. Lasting impressions of the nameless. Nostalgia to aid the passing of time. Brian Fanelli's collection celebrates the quiet triumphs of the underdog, gives due praise to the soft spoken dreams and iron will of the working class, and gives equal thought to roads traveled and others left in the dust. These poems explore what remains when youth has slipped into the past, when soldiers return from war, when it's better to hate a job than to have no job at all. *All That Remains* captures the hunger of the American Dream—even while speculating that the dream may no longer exist.

—Lori A May, author of *stains*
editor, *Poets' Quarterly*

Selected Titles Published by Unbound Content

A Bank Robber's Bad Luck With His Ex-Girlfriend
By KJ Hannah Greenberg

A Strange Frenzy
By Dom Gabrielli

At Age Twenty
By Maxwell Baumbach

Assumption
By Jim Davis

Before the Great Troubling
Our Locust Years
By Corey Mesler

Elegy
By Raphaela Willington

In New Jersey
By Julie Ellinger Hunt

Painting Czeslawa Kwoka: Honoring Children of the Holocaust
By Theresa Senato Edwards and Lori Schreiner

Saltian
By Alice Shapiro

The Pomegranate Papers
This is how honey runs
Wednesday
By Cassie Premo Steele

Written All Over Your Face{book}
By PMPope

Made in the USA
Charleston, SC
28 December 2013